Specific Skill Series

Using the Context

Richard A. Boning

Fifth Edition

SRA/McGraw-Hill
Columbus, Ohio

SRA/McGraw-Hill

A Division of The **McGraw·Hill** *Companies*

Printed in the United States of America.

Send all inquiries to:
    SRA/McGraw-Hill
    250 Old Wilson Bridge Road, Suite 310
    Worthington, OH 43085

ISBN 0-02-687944-1

    5 6 7 8 9 IMP 00 99

To the Teacher

PURPOSE:

USING THE CONTEXT has been designed to improve word comprehension and consequently comprehension in general. The reader's attention is directed to language patterns, word form, precise word usage, grammatical correctness, and word recognition. Most important of all, USING THE CONTEXT puts a premium on precise thinking.

FOR WHOM:

The skill of USING THE CONTEXT is developed through a series of books spanning ten levels (Picture, Preparatory, A, B, C, D, E, F, G, H). The Picture Level is for pupils who have not acquired a basic sight vocabulary. The Preparatory Level is for pupils who have a basic sight vocabulary but are not yet ready for the first-grade-level book. Books A through H are appropriate for pupils who can read on levels one through eight, respectively. **The use of the *Specific Skill Series Placement Test* is recommended to determine the appropriate level.**

THE NEW EDITION:

The fifth edition of the *Specific Skill Series* maintains the quality and focus that has distinguished this program for more than 25 years. A key element central to the program's success has been the unique nature of the reading selections. Nonfiction pieces about current topics have been designed to stimulate the interest of students, motivating them to use the comprehension strategies they have learned to further their reading. To keep this important aspect of the program intact, a percentage of the reading selections have been replaced in order to ensure the continued relevance of the subject material.

In addition, a significant percentage of the artwork in the program has been replaced to give the books a contemporary look. The cover photographs are designed to appeal to readers of all ages.

SESSIONS:

Short practice sessions are the most effective. It is desirable to have a practice session every day or every other day, using a few units each session.

SCORING:

Pupils should record their answers on the reproducible worksheets. The worksheets make scoring easier and provide uniform records of the pupils' work. Using worksheets also avoids consuming the exercise books.

It is important for pupils to know how well they are doing. For this reason, units should be scored as soon as they have been completed. Then a discussion can be held in which pupils justify their choices. (The Integrated Language Activities, many of which are open-ended, do not lend themselves to an objective score; thus there are no answer keys for these pages.)

GENERAL INFORMATION ON *USING THE CONTEXT*:

The meaning of the word *context* should be explained at the outset of instruction. At the earlier reading levels pupils should think of *context* as meaning the *neighborhood* in which a word lives. They should think of it as a clue in identifying new words. This concept can be expanded until the reader conceives of *context* in the fullest sense of the term.

Pupils must understand that it is not desirable to sacrifice accuracy of comprehension for speed. Without rigid time limits, readers can judge each possibility against the total context.

SUGGESTED STEPS:

1. Pupils read the passage. As they come to a missing word, they substitute the word *blank* in its place and proceed until they finish the passage.
2. After pupils read the entire passage, they determine the best choices. If the answers are not immediately obvious, pupils should try each of the choices before making a decision. Common types of incorrect choices include **nonpertinent choice, restricted-context choice, imprecise choice, ungrammatical choice**, and **confused-form choice**.
3. On the Picture Level, pupils read the sentence first. Then they choose the picture that represents the word needed to complete the sentence.

Additional information on using USING THE CONTEXT with pupils will be found in the **Specific Skill Series Teacher's Manual**.

RELATED MATERIALS:

Specific Skill Series Placement Tests, which enable the teacher to place pupils at their appropriate levels in each skill, are available for the Elementary (Pre-1–6) and Midway (4–8) grade levels.

About This Book

Often in your reading you will come across a difficult new word. You may be able to read the word, but you still do not know what it means. One way of finding out the word's meaning is by looking it up in a dictionary. Another way is to use **context**. You can think of context as being like a "neighborhood" in which the word "lives." A word is never alone. It appears in a sentence with other words, and the sentence has other sentences that come before and after it. These words and sentences are the context of the unknown word.

A word's context often contains clues to its meaning. To find clues, think about the meanings of the other words in that sentence. Look at the sentences that come before and after the sentence that contains the word. Do they give you any clues? Sometimes a writer gives an **example** that can help you figure out the word's meaning. Sometimes you may find a word that has almost the **same** meaning, or a word that means the **opposite**, or even a **definition** of the unfamiliar word, in the same sentence or a nearby one. These are all context clues.

Read the following sentence. Can you guess from the context what word might fit in the blank?

> We stopped rowing and drifted through the water in our new _____.

Did you guess from the context that the word was probably *boat*? If you did, you were able to tell from the other words in the sentence that the missing word must be a noun. You could also tell that the word names something that moves in the water. It is something that people might sit in. All these context clues helped you know that the word *boat* would make sense.

In this book you will read short paragraphs in which two words have been left out. Choose the correct word for each blank. Context clues in the paragraph will help you decide which words correctly complete the sentences.

Alcatraz is an island near San Francisco, California. It once housed the most dangerous of U.S. prisoners in five-by-nine foot cells. Although the prison was closed in 1963, Alcatraz is now open to tourists, who can (1) _____ scenes of the island's (2) _____.

1. **(A) space**   **(B) wade**   **(C) view**   **(D) votes**
2. **(A) birth**   **(B) past**   **(C) gold**   **(D) future**

Water takes three forms. It can be a liquid that can be (3) _____ from one place to another. When it is very cold, water turns to (4) _____ and is a solid. Water vapor, a gas, is the third form.

3. **(A) poured**   **(B) torn**   **(C) tried**   **(D) planned**
4. **(A) air**   **(B) raindrops**   **(C) ice**   **(D) color**

Look at the sleeves of people's suits. There you will see buttons that no longer "button." The buttons (5) _____ from the days of long ago when they were (6) _____ to hold back long, flowing cuffs.

5. **(A) foot**   **(B) remain**   **(C) listen**   **(D) such**
6. **(A) teach**   **(B) shiny**   **(C) tail**   **(D) used**

Can you picture dust chasing a mop? A mop that has been treated with chemicals will absorb dust quickly. The dust seems to run after it. Such a mop (7) _____ something like a (8) _____.

7. **(A) under**   **(B) blue**   **(C) well**   **(D) works**
8. **(A) goat**   **(B) doors**   **(C) magnet**   **(D) drum**

Members of the United States Coast Guard make up the police force of the sea. They ride in (9) _____ rather than cars. Their job is to make certain that the (10) _____ of the sea are obeyed.

9. **(A) chains**   **(B) fools**   **(C) crabs**   **(D) boats**
10. **(A) broom**   **(B) teeth**   **(C) laws**   **(D) ships**

The Young Visitors is a book that pokes fun at English society during the early 1900s. When published, over 200,000 (11) _____ of the book were sold. Surprisingly, it was (12) _____ by a nine-year-old girl who never wrote another book!

11. (A) needles   (B) stones   (C) copies   (D) places
12. (A) towed   (B) written   (C) plowed   (D) bathed

Haiku is a special type of poem. It is three lines long and has seventeen syllables (13) _____. The first line usually has five syllables. The (14) _____ line has seven, and the third has five syllables.

13. (A) alone   (B) once   (C) altogether   (D) everyday
14. (A) beginning   (B) end   (C) second   (D) shortest

Lobsters are caught in wooden traps called "pots." The traps are (15) _____ with (16) _____. Then they are lowered to the ocean bottom by ropes. Lobsters find the traps easy to get into, but difficult to get out of.

15. (A) baited   (B) travel   (C) school   (D) meant
16. (A) train   (B) nest   (C) fish   (D) clear

Insects can be found almost everywhere. They buzz around high mountain peaks and thrive in swampy marshes or deep caves. But few insects are found near the (17) _____ since they do not like (18) _____ water.

17. (A) ocean   (B) hills   (C) farm   (D) porch
18. (A) pretty   (B) soft   (C) salt   (D) blue

The alligator is not a fussy eater. Not long ago, a bull alligator swallowed a live, five-foot rattlesnake. Although the alligator got a sore mouth from rattlesnake poison, it seemed to (19) _____ its (20) _____.

19. (A) dislike   (B) scatter   (C) enjoy   (D) catch
20. (A) meal   (B) swim   (C) game   (D) hobby

How could Jennifer Nelson win a spelling contest without even hearing the (1) _____ pronounced? Jennifer, who had been deaf since she was 1½ years old, was clever enough to (2) _____ the lips of the teacher who was saying the words.

1. (A) sticks	(B) bells	(C) smell	(D) words
2. (A) color	(B) listen	(C) read	(D) change

What is the combination of the lock at Fort Knox, where our country's gold is stored? No one person knows. Each person knows a (3) _____ of the combination. The lock will (4) _____ only when all the parts are dialed.

3. (A) map	(B) part	(C) dance	(D) season
4. (A) fasten	(B) open	(C) rust	(D) flame

Some of nature's most beautiful animals cannot be seen with the naked eye. Were it not for the microscope, a long parade of (5) _____ life would be completely (6) _____ from human sight.

5. (A) rock	(B) animal	(C) clowns	(D) rocks
6. (A) hidden	(B) most	(C) space	(D) tune

Coin collectors touch their coins only with care. If a collector (7) _____ a coin, he or she holds it by the edges, never flat on the palm. Moisture from the (8) _____ could stain the coin.

7. (A) throws	(B) sells	(C) handles	(D) finds
8. (A) wallet	(B) hand	(C) rain	(D) dust

When most people are asked if they would like a blue steak or a glass of olive-green milk, their mouths turn down. "No, indeed!" they (9) _____. Certain (10) _____ are not too appealing in foods.

9. (A) loose	(B) eat	(C) take	(D) reply
10. (A) colors	(B) rocks	(C) open	(D) nest

Cherokee Indians knew a special way to catch fish. They threw certain plants into a stream. These plants stunned the fish. Not able to swim, the fish floated to the (11) _____, and the Cherokee (12) _____ them.

11. (A) clouds   (B) surface   (C) balloon   (D) dust
12. (A) swam   (B) played   (C) collected   (D) filled

Sea turtles never lose their sense of direction. When they hatch from eggs laid on the sand, they crawl right out to the ocean. Even when carried to a new place, they always (13) _____ their way back to the (14) _____.

13. (A) lose   (B) grow   (C) find   (D) drink
14. (A) book   (B) sea   (C) arena   (D) fish

Can you picture a tree with more than one trunk? The banyan tree of India has hundreds of trunks. One banyan tree (15) _____ like a (16) _____ of many trees.

15. (A) tastes   (B) looks   (C) finds   (D) branch
16. (A) meal   (B) leaf   (C) left   (D) forest

In 1930, Ruth G. Wakefield ran out of baker's chocolate at her inn in Massachusetts. She tried to make chocolate cookies by cutting chocolate bits and dropping them into regular cookie (17) _____ . Instead, Wakefield (18) _____ the chocolate chip cookie.

17. (A) smoke   (B) fuel   (C) dough   (D) dye
18. (A) destroyed   (B) created   (C) mailed   (D) wasted

The blind can tell time with special clocks. The clocks have raised dots for each number. A blind person can (19) _____ the dots and the (20) _____ of the clock, to find out what time it is.

19. (A) feel   (B) seen   (C) letter   (D) clean
20. (A) feet   (B) hands   (C) cook   (D) smile

Admiral Robert E. Peary reached the North Pole in 1909 after spending twenty years (1) _____ the Arctic. He started out with 23 other men and 133 dogs. But, most of the party had turned back before reaching the Pole because of a (2) _____ of supplies.

1. **(A) hiding**   **(B) thinking**   **(C) mining**   **(D) exploring**
2. **(A) lack**   **(B) truck**   **(C) lot**   **(D) massive**

Long ago, people got their last names from the jobs they held. A person who prepared food got the name (3) _____. A person who worked with wood came to be called (4) _____.

3. **(A) Cook**   **(B) Car**   **(C) Plumber**   **(D) Pot**
4. **(A) Smith**   **(B) Baker**   **(C) Tooth**   **(D) Carpenter**

Water lilies in the Amazon Valley grow very large. When children sit on these huge, firm leaves, the lilies look more like (5) _____ than floating (6) _____.

5. **(A) rafts**   **(B) coal**   **(C) people**   **(D) children**
6. **(A) trees**   **(B) flowers**   **(C) rivers**   **(D) rocks**

Hetty Green, one of the (7) _____ women in the world, didn't believe in spending money. She dressed her children in secondhand clothes, lived in run-down houses, and went everywhere in an old black dress and rubber boots stuffed with money. She (8) _____ leaving one hundred million dollars.

7. **(A) loveliest**   **(B) richest**   **(C) neediest**   **(D) kindest**
8. **(A) partied**   **(B) shopped**   **(C) died**   **(D) entertained**

Is the banana the oldest fruit on earth? Many scientists believe that it is. They say that bananas first (9) _____ in Asia where early people carried banana roots from place to place. Today the banana is a favorite (10) _____ around the world.

9. **(A) fooled**   **(B) met**   **(C) spoke**   **(D) grew**
10. **(A) twin**   **(B) fruit**   **(C) pool**   **(D) meat**

The Indian Botanical Garden in Calcutta has a tree to brag about. A banyan there has the largest circumference recorded. It is 1,350 feet (11) _____ . It covers three acres and has (12) _____ there for at least 200 years.

11. **(A) around**   **(B) high**   **(C) long**   **(D) old**
12. **(A) died**   **(B) run**   **(C) stood**   **(D) laughed**

"Black diamonds" are not really diamonds at all. They are black but are much larger than diamonds. Found underground in (13) _____ black diamonds are really lumps of (14) _____ .

13. **(A) mines**   **(B) water**   **(C) shelters** **(D) wells**
14. **(A) cereal**   **(B) coal**   **(C) ice**   **(D) bread**

Have you lost your cat? One has been found. There is an ad in the local (15) _____ . If it is your cat, please (16) _____ it. The cat wants to go home.

15. **(A) house**   **(B) newspaper** **(C) fence**   **(D) box**
16. **(A) claim**   **(B) mend**   **(C) build**   **(D) tear**

A thunderstorm changed the course of history. Because the battlefield was muddy, Napoleon's army was forced to slow down. This gave the Prussians time to (17) _____ on the battlefield. Together with the English, they (18) _____ Napoleon at Waterloo.

17. **(A) sleep**   **(B) wash**   **(C) arrive**   **(D) eat**
18. **(A) sold**   **(B) defeated** **(C) fled**   **(D) protected**

Carlsbad Caverns in New Mexico has a limestone cave called the Big Room. It is nearly (19) _____ enough for the Statue of Liberty to stand up in. And it is as (20) _____ as twelve football fields laid side by side.

19. **(A) full**   **(B) tall**   **(C) light**   **(D) small**
20. **(A) quiet**   **(B) thin**   **(C) wide**   **(D) noisy**

The skeletons of most animals are hidden by flesh and skin. Insects wear their skeletons for all to see. Nature arranged for the tiny (1) _____ to wear its skeleton on the (2) _____ .

1. (A) insect   (B) test   (C) tell   (D) love
2. (A) carpet   (B) board   (C) outside   (D) thin

Handkerchiefs were once round instead of square. Almost two hundred years ago, a French king said that all handkerchiefs must be square. A (3) _____ was started by a (4) _____ .

3. (A) fashion   (B) elephant   (C) letter   (D) garden
4. (A) law   (B) fast   (C) machine   (D) much

Long ago, people traded for what they wanted. A family with six cows might give milk to a fishing family and get fish in (5) _____ . This kind of (6) _____ is called "barter."

5. (A) January   (B) return   (C) season   (D) size
6. (A) banking   (B) stealing   (C) meaning   (D) trading

People of long ago had only first names. As the population grew, people began to live in larger groups. Families started to use last names. These (7) _____ names helped people (8) _____ one another more easily.

7. (A) family   (B) animal   (C) foreign   (D) battle
8. (A) catch   (B) feed   (C) fall   (D) identify

People who watch television like to snack. On the average, the chance of becoming overweight increases by two percent for each hour a person (9) _____ daily in front of the television (10) _____ .

9. (A) yells   (B) hunts   (C) spends   (D) sings
10. (A) magazine   (B) truck   (C) schedule   (D) screen

UNIT 4

Did you know that about one out of every ten Americans plays the piano? Even though it is a favorite (11) _____ in this country, the United States does not lead in the making of pianos. Japan (12) _____ more pianos than any other country in the world.

11. **(A) vinegar**   **(B) instrument**   **(C) sword**   **(D) highway**
12. **(A) starves**   **(B) amuses**   **(C) makes**   **(D) burns**

Eyeglasses were an important invention. Over 125,000,000 people in America now (13) _____ them! Two out of every three adults in the country are among this number. Another ten million or more children and adults use contact lenses to help them see (14) _____.

13. **(A) tame**   **(B) stir**   **(C) lash**   **(D) wear**
14. **(A) worse**   **(B) better**   **(C) sorry**   **(D) awful**

Modern women like to own many different kinds of shoes. Back in the year 1500, women liked to (15) _____ many pairs of gloves. Queen Elizabeth I owned about 1,000 (16) _____.

15. **(A) own**   **(B) fancy**   **(C) swim**   **(D) smile**
16. **(A) cats**   **(B) pairs**   **(C) servants**   **(D) ships**

Some fish do not have manners. The archerfish spits into the air. It hits insects that are flying two feet above the water. The archer's manners may be poor, but its (17) _____ is (18) _____.

17. **(A) smile**   **(B) pond**   **(C) aim**   **(D) yard**
18. **(A) sad**   **(B) cold**   **(C) below**   **(D) perfect**

A shoe must fit the foot that wears it. If the shoe does not fit, it changes the shape of the foot. The foot may become quite sore. It is (19) _____ to (20) _____ a shoe that fits.

19. **(A) floor**   **(B) found**   **(C) never**   **(D) best**
20. **(A) send**   **(B) mark**   **(C) buy**   **(D) drop**

UNIT 5

The bottle tree grows in Australia. The trunk of the tree is shaped like a bottle. The branches look like flowers sticking out of a (1) _____ . People always (2) _____ to look at this unusual tree.

1. (A) car   (B) bottle   (C) corn   (D) night
2. (A) stop   (B) tent   (C) play   (D) rake

The slimy snail is an amazing creature. The leathery skin of its foot is so (3) _____ that it can climb over the (4) _____ of a sharp blade without hurting itself.

3. (A) swim   (B) red   (C) tough   (D) candle
4. (A) night   (B) writing   (C) blue   (D) edge

For years, people thought the giraffe could not make a sound. One day a zookeeper overheard a soft mooing and became aware that the giraffe makes a (5) _____ like a (6) _____ .

5. (A) kite   (B) shower   (C) sudden   (D) sound
6. (A) pig   (B) cow   (C) mouse   (D) bird

In Asia, parts of different animals are used for medicine. Deer antlers are pounded into dust and (7) _____ to keep body tissues from aging. Crocodile scales are (8) _____ in butter and used to cure toothaches and boils!

7. (A) climbed   (B) scolded   (C) hissed   (D) used
8. (A) shouted   (B) obeyed   (C) cooked   (D) smiled

In 1944, Margaret Whiting sang "Moonlight in Vermont" and made the song famous. Surprisingly, Whiting was not from Vermont and had never been there. Forty years (9) _____ she finally (10) _____ the state and was made an "honorary Vermonter."

9. (A) earlier   (B) sooner   (C) before   (D) later
10. (A) left   (B) named   (C) visited   (D) captured

A horse named Butterscotch actually drove a car! It turned a switch and pulled a lever with its mouth. Then Butterscotch (11) _____ on the gas pedal. As the car moved forward, the horse turned the steering (12) _____ with its nose.

11. (A) stepped   (B) barked   (C) starved   (D) blinked
12. (A) dollar   (B) garage   (C) wheel   (D) kettle

The largest eyes in the world are those of the mighty blue whale. Like grapefruits, these eyes are in keeping with the (13) _____ of the whale. It's fortunate that whales don't wear (14) _____.

13. (A) feet   (B) radio   (C) orange   (D) size
14. (A) sad   (B) eyeglasses   (C) trunk   (D) tree

Fish farms are carefully tended, just as are regular farms on land. Dirt walls are built around fields. The fields are (15) _____ and stocked with (16) _____. Within a year the fish "crop" is fully grown.

15. (A) flooded   (B) rolled   (C) bitten   (D) speed
16. (A) butter   (B) fish   (C) glass   (D) tables

Tornadoes are powerful windstorms. They often destroy everything in their paths, but sometimes they can be gentle. One tornado (17) _____ up a (18) _____ of pickles. The full jar was found, unbroken, in a ditch twenty-five miles away!

17. (A) crept   (B) picked   (C) paid   (D) chopped
18. (A) cake   (B) jar   (C) tribe   (D) list

Scientists are looking for ways to use the sea as farmers use the land. They say it might be possible to herd fish just as (19) _____ herd (20) _____. More meat for everyone would result.

19. (A) dentist   (B) stores   (C) ranchers   (D) paper
20. (A) rope   (B) prices   (C) nose   (D) cattle

Save pennies and get rich. Start by saving one penny. The next day, save twice that (1) _____, or two pennies. On the third day, (2) _____ four pennies. Save twice the amount from the day before for one month and you'll have over five million dollars!

1. (A) jungle   (B) diamond   (C) amount   (D) advice
2. (A) choke   (B) tear   (C) nibble   (D) save

Considering its size, the tiny flea can out jump a person. Seven- and ten-inch jumps are common. For humans to do as well for their size, a 400-foot jump would be necessary. The (3) _____ is quite an (4) _____.

3. (A) rain   (B) flea   (C) trunk   (D) lion
4. (A) eater   (B) artist   (C) athlete   (D) toad

The world's tallest lady lives alone. Do not feel (5) _____ for her as she has many (6) _____ each day. As tall as a ten-story building, she is the famous Statue of Liberty.

5. (A) jump   (B) happy   (C) sorry   (D) friendly
6. (A) visitors   (B) pains   (C) toys   (D) hours

Plains Indians used beetles to help make wooden pipes. A beetle would eat its way through a wooden stick. After the beetle had hollowed out the stick, the (7) _____ would have a new (8) _____ to use.

7. (A) Plains Indians   (B) giants   (C) moon   (D) enemies
8. (A) dog   (B) pipe   (C) lasso   (D) plate

A surprising number of people give animals to the zoo. Sometimes owners tire of their pets. Most often these pets have grown too large to be taken care of properly. After (9) _____, zoos get many (10) _____ as gifts.

9. (A) mope   (B) dawn   (C) Easter   (D) poles
10. (A) traffic   (B) leaves   (C) people   (D) rabbits

An ostrich will eat almost anything. A rock or stone tastes fine to this bird. A watch (11) _____ out of someone's (12) _____ is swallowed with delight. What is most surprising, the ostrich never has a stomach ache!

11. **(A) tree**   **(B) tight**   **(C) picked**   **(D) made**
12. **(A) pocket**   **(B) foot**   **(C) plane**   **(D) silver**

Before the American Revolution, people in the colonies used the money of other countries. One coin that was used was the Spanish dollar. When (13) _____ was needed, this coin was cut into eight pieces. Each one-eighth of the dollar was (14) _____ as a "bit."

13. **(A) change**   **(B) bill**   **(C) checks**   **(D) tickets**
14. **(A) thrown**   **(B) known**   **(C) sent**   **(D) claimed**

After car accidents, falls are the second most common (15) _____ of accidental death in the U.S. Most people fall on home stairs. Their falls usually happen on the first three or last three (16) _____.

15. **(A) cause**   **(B) argument**   **(C) title**   **(D) sport**
16. **(A) steps**   **(B) railings**   **(C) legs**   **(D) feet**

Whiskers are helpful to certain animals. A tiger hunting in the (17) _____ uses its whiskers to help it feel its way through the brush. Cats and rats also use their whiskers to (18) _____ them while chasing enemies.

17. **(A) forest**   **(B) traffic**   **(C) city**   **(D) telescope**
18. **(A) clap**   **(B) jump**   **(C) drown**   **(D) guide**

Have you ever noticed that suit jackets have slits in the back? Years ago many people rode horses. The slit allowed the riders to spread their coattails while (19) _____. The slit (20) _____ in suit jackets to this day.

19. **(A) talking**   **(B) riding**   **(C) visiting**   **(D) dressing**
20. **(A) laughs**   **(B) short**   **(C) remains**   **(D) takes**

A. Exercising Your Skill

Sometimes when you read, you will see a word you do not know. How can you find out what an unknown word means? One way is to look for clues in the words and sentences around the word. This is called using the **context**. One kind of context clue is found in the meanings of other words that you *do* know. Another kind of context clue is found in words with similar meanings, or *synonyms*.

Read the paragraph below. As you read, look for clues to the meanings of the underlined words. On your paper, write each underlined word. Tell what you think each word means. Then tell what clues you used to figure out each word's meaning.

A desert is a place where rain <u>seldom</u> falls. It might rain only once in four or more years. The camel is well suited to its <u>arid</u> desert home. A camel can go for about eight days without water. Its feet are <u>broad</u> and have soft pads. These wide feet do not sink into the sand. <u>Double</u> eyelashes protect the camel's eyes from sandstorms. These two rows of lashes keep sand from entering the camel's eyes.

B. Expanding Your Skill

Some of the clues you used to figure out the meanings of the underlined words in Part A were synonyms. The words *broad* and *wide* are synonyms. They have almost the same meaning. Can you think of synonyms for other words in the paragraph? Talk about it with your classmates. See how many synonyms you can find for *seldom*, *arid*, *broad*, and *double*.

C. Exploring Language

Read this story. Find the words that do *not* make sense in the context of the story. Then think of words that would make more sense in those sentences. Rewrite the sentences using the new words.

A desert is a place of many contrasts. In the daytime, it can be very hot. At night, the temperature can rise well below freezing. For most of the year, little rain falls in the desert. But sometimes, it will rain so lightly that the land is flooded. At first glance, a desert sounds like an empty place. Look more closely, though, and you will find few living things. Many snakes, lizards, birds, and other fish live in the desert.

D. Expressing Yourself

Choose one of these activities.

1. Think of words you could replace in one of the paragraphs on these two pages. Brainstorm with your classmates to think of other words that would fit the context. Choose two or three sentences to rewrite, using the new words.

2. Use reference books to find out more about the desert and its animal and plant life. Write a paragraph that tells what you have learned.

3. Imagine that you are a travel agent. Write an ad that will interest people in a desert vacation. Draw a picture to illustrate your ad.

Most of the Earth's surface is covered by water. Less than a third is covered by soil. Perhaps our planet should be called "Ocean" instead of Earth. It is (1) _____ a (2) _____ planet.

1. (A) truly   (B) up   (C) around   (D) down
2. (A) skinny   (B) fuzzy   (C) watery   (D) dry

"Watch your step, please!" says the new talking elevator. The elevator calls out floor numbers and makes other announcements. It seems strange to (3) _____ an elevator (4) _____.

3. (A) paint   (B) hear   (C) ride   (D) hold
4. (A) speak   (B) hill   (C) home   (D) bell

Winter brings hardships to our winged friends. While some birds can stand very cold weather, they cannot always find food. Even more important is their need for water. In winter, birds (5) _____ your (6) _____.

5. (A) fly   (B) need   (C) sing   (D) hop
6. (A) help   (B) house   (C) cage   (D) coat

The bulging eyes of the mudskipper fish can get sunburned if the fish swims close to the surface. To (7) _____ this from (8) _____, the mudskipper turns its eyes right around in their sockets!

7. (A) prevent   (B) cure   (C) trip   (D) make
8. (A) sleep   (B) lamp   (C) happening   (D) going

In 1868, a monstrous wave caused sixteen ships to be wrecked near the country of Wales. The huge wave had been (9) _____ by an earthquake five thousand miles (10) _____ in South America.

9. (A) watched   (B) created   (C) stopped   (D) frozen
10. (A) away   (B) late   (C) near   (D) overhead

Horses known as "throw backs" scare even the bravest of cowhands. Such horses throw themselves (11) _____ in an effort to shake their (12) _____. The cowhand who must ride a "throw back" is very unlucky.

11.	(A) money	(B) backward	(C) down	(D) food
12.	(A) ground	(B) skin	(C) riders	(D) young

People can now ski indoors. An indoor ski slope of nylon "snow" has been developed. Skiers zip down the slope at any (13) _____ of the year, without regard for the (14) _____.

13.	(A) snow	(B) heard	(C) time	(D) slope
14.	(A) weather	(B) ski	(C) chair	(D) feet

The Incas of South America had an unusual way of solving arithmetic problems. They used knotted strings and could (15) _____ and (16) _____ with amazing speed. These strings are still in use today.

15.	(A) run	(B) multiply	(C) repeat	(D) talk
16.	(A) join	(B) throw	(C) jump	(D) divide

Insects have blood, too. Their blood isn't bright red like people's blood. Insect blood has no (17) _____. Sometimes, when insects are hit, bright red blood (18) _____ from them. That's just blood that the insects have sucked from people.

17.	(A) fur	(B) color	(C) holiday	(D) beard
18.	(A) squeezes	(B) whispers	(C) tastes	(D) pedals

Of all the insects in the world, none is more beautiful than the (19) _____. Its silklike wings flash rainbow colors in the sunlight. (20) _____ gracefully from flower to flower, it is a fascinating insect to watch.

19.	(A) worm	(B) spider	(C) crow	(D) butterfly
20.	(A) Flying	(B) Driving	(C) Calling	(D) Throwing

UNIT 8

Robots are (1) _____ that can do the work of people. They build and paint cars, run other machines, pick up chocolates and put them in boxes, and shear sheep. One robot even (2) _____ a band.

1. (A) sidewalks   (B) machines   (C) valleys   (D) syllables
2. (A) smoked   (B) grumbled   (C) directed   (D) envied

Many years ago a piper walked through the streets of Hamelin, Germany. According to the story, the piper's magic music charmed millions of rats. The piper cleverly led the rats to the (3) _____. All the rats drowned and the (4) _____ of Hamelin rejoiced.

3. (A) river   (B) houses   (C) desert   (D) moon
4. (A) rats   (B) people   (C) cheese   (D) egg

People who like to eat often try to set eating records. The champion eater of all time (5) _____ fourteen hard-boiled eggs in less than one minute. Another person broke a (6) _____ by eating over twenty hamburgers with buns in three minutes.

5. (A) cooked   (B) equipped   (C) speckled   (D) ate
6. (A) record   (B) pitcher   (C) mirror   (D) board

A bloodhound is used to track down criminals. This dog, with its keen sense of smell, can easily pick up the trail of a criminal. Many criminals (7) _____ the bloodhound more than the (8) _____.

7. (A) love   (B) pet   (C) fear   (D) week
8. (A) basket   (B) police   (C) sickness   (D) teachers

The sea rabbit is a strange fish. It looks something like a (9) _____ but cannot hop about with its one foot. This (10) _____ smells with its ear and hears with its foot!

9. (A) clocks   (B) cow   (C) pig   (D) rabbit
10. (A) fish   (B) snake   (C) boat   (D) horse

"Welcome Stranger" is the name of a gold nugget. It (11) _____ two hundred and ten pounds. This nugget is said to be the largest piece of (12) _____ ever found.

11. **(A) meets**   **(B) shines**   **(C) break**   **(D) weighs**
12. **(A) gold**   **(B) silver**   **(C) paper**   **(D) coal**

The hydra, a tiny freshwater cousin of the jellyfish, has a poisonous sting. But Dr. Georgia Lesh-Laurie found a (13) _____ in the poison of the sting that (14) _____ the heartbeat of humans.

13. **(A) hobby**   **(B) question**   **(C) welcome**   **(D) material**
14. **(A) tastes**   **(B) improves**   **(C) includes**   **(D) wastes**

It takes millions of years for decaying plants to change into coal. It takes very little time for coal to burn. Too bad it takes but a few minutes to (15) _____ and millions of years to (16) _____ .

15. **(A) study**   **(B) buy**   **(C) burn**   **(D) forget**
16. **(A) learn**   **(B) form**   **(C) dark**   **(D) run**

The remora fish will grab hold of a passing shark for a free ride. The remora then gets a free (17) _____ while riding along. It snatches the food that drops from the (18) _____ of the shark.

17. **(A) ticket**   **(B) book**   **(C) kisses**   **(D) meal**
18. **(A) big**   **(B) mouth**   **(C) round**   **(D) side**

Everything in Texas comes king-sized. Some of the ranches are very large. One, named the King Ranch, covers 825,000 acres. This is about one third as (19) _____ as the (20) _____ of Delaware.

19. **(A) large**   **(B) piece**   **(C) hour**   **(D) slow**
20. **(A) month**   **(B) climate**   **(C) clock**   **(D) state**

Most people (1) _____ about eight hours of sleep a night. How would you (2) _____ if you never got any sleep? Al Herpin lived to be ninety-four years old and never slept. Doctors discovered that Al rested by sitting in a rocking chair and reading.

1. (A) punish   (B) hoe   (C) copy   (D) need
2. (A) intend   (B) feel   (C) ring   (D) die

Jeff Hudson, the world's tiniest person, was eighteen inches tall. One day he was put into a pie which was set before the Queen of England. As Jeff jumped out, the Queen (3) _____ with (4) _____.

3. (A) wrote   (B) watched   (C) send   (D) apple
4. (A) rest   (B) hope   (C) mouse   (D) surprise

In the late 1600s, Mary Mundy of England was engaged to be married. When the man she planned to marry caught a cold and (5) _____, she built a fireplace to honor his (6) _____.

5. (A) rested   (B) sighed   (C) voted   (D) died
6. (A) courage   (B) memory   (C) kindness   (D) future

Shoe sizes run from "A" to "E." (Sounds like a report card, doesn't it?) A double "E" is very wide. A double "A" is very narrow. "C" would not be very (7) _____ or very (8) _____.

7. (A) old   (B) pretty   (C) wide   (D) tight
8. (A) new   (B) fine   (C) narrow   (D) clever

Years ago in the country of Siam, white elephants were given large palaces in which to live. The elephants were not only (9) _____ with servants, but even had their (10) _____ served on beautiful tablecloths!

9. (A) watered   (B) beaten   (C) pushed   (D) provided
10. (A) monkeys   (B) lions   (C) meals   (D) tables

If someone is said to "have a mint," it means that the person has much money. A mint is a place where money is made. Wouldn't it be nice if every person could have a (11) _____ of one's (12) _____?

11. (A) sight   (B) nose   (C) bank   (D) mint
12. (A) friend   (B) own   (C) house   (D) safe

For centuries people in Europe paid no attention to the potato. Then they found out that one acre of potatoes could (13) _____ a family of (14) _____ for a whole year! With this discovery, the lowly potato won lasting fame.

13. (A) force   (B) feed   (C) teach   (D) work
14. (A) lettuce   (B) four   (C) plants   (D) insects

Many states in our country have been given Native-American names, but the names have often been (15) _____ from the way they were spoken by the Native Americans. "Neb-rathka" is now (16) _____. "Quinnehtukqut" is now Connecticut.

15. (A) gone   (B) liked   (C) changed   (D) traded
16. (A) Maine   (B) Newton   (C) Idaho   (D) Nebraska

One million tons of gold are scattered throughout the oceans of the world. Whoever can find an easy and inexpensive way to separate the (17) _____ from the (18) _____ will become wealthy beyond belief.

17. (A) gold   (B) wood   (C) sky   (D) salt
18. (A) fish   (B) plants   (C) water   (D) wheat

People once had the notion that clothing could be made out of spider webs. The idea was soon dropped. It was realized that 600,000 spiders were (19) _____ to (20) _____ just one pound of silk.

19. (A) kissed   (B) needed   (C) tasted   (D) spent
20. (A) produce   (B) deliver   (C) carry   (D) sell

Canada, the large country that lies north of the United States, got its name from the Iroquois. The Iroquois (1) _____ *kanata* or *kanada* (2) _____ "village" or "group of huts."

1. (A) food   (B) word   (C) trail   (D) arrow
2. (A) leads   (B) flies   (C) means   (D) grows

A dream machine can help anyone bothered by nightmares. The machine (3) _____ an alarm when the sleeper takes twenty-five or more breaths a minute. A (4) _____ breathing that quickly is about to begin a terrible nightmare.

3. (A) sounds   (B) shovels   (C) tastes   (D) drinks
4. (A) dollar   (B) sleeper   (C) skeleton   (D) kettle

Try holding your breath. It is not easy to hold it for more than a minute or two. If you give up quickly, you will never (5) _____ the world's (6) _____. One American took a breath and held it for fourteen minutes.

5. (A) stick   (B) drop   (C) set   (D) pick
6. (A) pencil   (B) record   (C) travel   (D) teeth

Our grandparents say, "Winters were colder when we were young." They are right. Winters are (7) _____ what they (8) _____ to be. For the past fifty years winters have been getting warmer.

7. (A) not   (B) under   (C) lost   (D) asking
8. (A) used   (B) left   (C) found   (D) want

As the hermit crab grows, its shell becomes too tight. Then it looks for the old shell of another sea creature. The hermit crab may try on (9) _____ shells before it finds one that will (10) _____.

9. (A) trick   (B) several   (C) shoes   (D) glasses
10. (A) talk   (B) sing   (C) fit   (D) shrink

The common cold is our number-one sickness. United States health reports show that about 200,000,000 school days are (11) _____ in one year as a (12) _____ of the common cold.

| 11. | (A) found | (B) lost | (C) seen | (D) told |
| 12. | (A) result | (B) sale | (C) game | (D) picture |

In the last century, ice farming was a big business. Ice was cut in the (13) _____ and stored in sheds. Sawdust helped keep the ice from (14) _____. Ice from Boston was a favorite in hot lands such as China and India.

| 13. | (A) heat | (B) excitement | (C) winter | (D) summer |
| 14. | (A) steaming | (B) freezing | (C) melting | (D) lakes |

Whales living in cold water have a thick coat of fat which serves as a warm overcoat. The fat, or blubber, of whales living in (15) _____ water is not nearly so (16) _____.

| 15. | (A) big | (B) little | (C) tall | (D) warmer |
| 16. | (A) red | (B) brave | (C) cute | (D) thick |

Birds have special calls to warn each other of danger. Although the warning calls differ with each type of bird, all birds understand one another. A cry of (17) _____ from one will send all flying to (18) _____.

| 17. | (A) alarm | (B) spin | (C) soap | (D) fight |
| 18. | (A) safety | (B) school | (C) hop | (D) jail |

Cats had a pleasant life in Egypt many years ago. They were treated with great care. Anyone who killed a cat was (19) _____ of a serious (20) _____.

| 19. | (A) guilty | (B) sold | (C) made | (D) wet |
| 20. | (A) crime | (B) meal | (C) garden | (D) story |

Before bicycles had pedals, riders would walk and glide, walk and glide. It wasn't until 1839 that pedals were (1) _____ to make constant (2) _____ possible.

1. (A) blocked   (B) added   (C) stored   (D) removed
2. (A) noise   (B) thought   (C) motion   (D) beauty

Do you ever wonder how far away a thunderstorm is? As soon as you see lightning, count the seconds until you hear thunder. For every five (3) _____ the (4) _____ is one mile away.

3. (A) pupils   (B) seconds   (C) drop   (D) day
4. (A) storm   (B) weather   (C) cloud   (D) road

There isn't one person on earth who does not travel one and a half million miles each day. That is the distance our earth (5) _____ through (6) _____ every twenty-four hours.

5. (A) zooms   (B) wades   (C) box   (D) calls
6. (A) water   (B) space   (C) stars   (D) roads

You have probably heard the saying "Barking dogs never bite." There isn't any truth to it. Many people have been bitten by barking dogs and have the (7) _____ marks to (8) _____ it.

7. (A) growth   (B) footprint   (C) passing   (D) teeth
8. (A) tame   (B) sign   (C) prove   (D) sailor

The sloth, a South American animal, hardly moves. Work of any kind does not interest it. It does so (9) _____ that its name has come to be used when talking about (10) _____ or slothful people.

9. (A) cat   (B) run   (C) little   (D) eat
10. (A) busy   (B) helpful   (C) active   (D) lazy

What was the most perfect boat ever built? Many boat designers (11) _____ that it was the birch-bark (12) _____ of the Native Americans. For grace, beauty, and perfection of design, this canoe has never been equaled.

11. **(A) disagree**   **(B) agree**   **(C) draw**   **(D) suffer**
12. **(A) sailboat**   **(B) canoe**   **(C) raft**   **(D) rowboat**

Cowhands catch wild horses in a clever way. They build a corral around a water hole. When the (13) _____ horses come for a (14) _____, the cowhand hiding nearby jerks the gate closed.

13. **(A) large**   **(B) tame**   **(C) thirsty**   **(D) white**
14. **(A) joke**   **(B) fight**   **(C) rest**   **(D) drink**

Chicago may be called the "Windy City," but it isn't the windiest place in the United States. New York City, New York, and Dodge City, Kansas, are windier. The (15) _____ place of all is Mount Washington, New Hampshire, where average winds (16) _____ at 35 miles per hour.

15. **(A) windiest**   **(B) funniest**   **(C) warmest**   **(D) deepest**
16. **(A) blow**   **(B) sell**   **(C) invent**   **(D) bubble**

We often use the expression "as fast as lightning." Do we know how fast lightning really is? Divide one second into ten thousand parts. A (17) _____ of lightning lasts as (18) _____ as one of these parts.

17. **(A) coat**   **(B) flash**   **(C) dream**   **(D) day**
18. **(A) long**   **(B) rope**   **(C) large**   **(D) small**

People often say "the four corners of the world" when they mean all parts of the world. However, as all of us know, the world is round. To have (19) _____ it would have to be (20) _____.

19. **(A) size**   **(B) weight**   **(C) corners**   **(D) food**
20. **(A) tall**   **(B) heavy**   **(C) square**   **(D) hidden**

In Europe, window boxes (1) _____ many city homes and apartments. Nearly every block is brightened by window-box gardens. Tulips, geraniums, black-eyed Susans, cherry tomatoes, small roses, Scotch bloom, and many other plants add (2) _____ and beauty.

1. (A) destroy   (B) decorate   (C) honk   (D) blame
2. (A) boards   (B) curtains   (C) color   (D) noise

Can you identify counterfeit money? It is not difficult. Counterfeit coins feel oily and make a dull sound when dropped. The edges of the coins are uneven. (3) _____ for these signs. Don't be (4) _____!

3. (A) Cheer   (B) Speak   (C) Watch   (D) Talk
4. (A) rude   (B) true   (C) happy   (D) fooled

Some animals can stand the bitter cold. Snails, for example, can be frozen at fifty degrees below zero and still (5) _____ to good health. There are many sturdy little creatures on (6) _____.

5. (A) walk   (B) pray   (C) return   (D) listen
6. (A) earth   (B) games   (C) clouds   (D) Mars

People pay high prices for fresh, uncooked fish eggs to eat. Eggs from a fish called the sturgeon are known as caviar. Such raw eggs (7) _____ fresh in a (8) _____ for only two or three weeks.

7. (A) color   (B) turn   (C) remain   (D) appear
8. (A) birdhouse   (B) refrigerator   (C) report   (D) stream

---

Cowhands were proud of their hats. They didn't like to take them off. They would wear them while eating and dancing. Sometimes, when out on the prairie at night, cowhands would even (9) _____ with their (10) _____ on.

9. (A) turn   (B) see   (C) sleep   (D) run
10. (A) boots   (B) glasses   (C) blankets   (D) hats

Snacks don't have to be junk food. Buy fresh and dried fruits, nuts, and cheeses. Carrot sticks and other raw vegetables are especially (11) _____ when dipped in a (12) _____ of cottage cheese, yogurt, and seasonings. Frozen orange juice pops are delicious.

11. (A) dirty	(B) tasty	(C) dangerous	(D) plain
12. (A) thread	(B) battle	(C) faucet	(D) mixture

The ancient Greeks used large keys to lock and (13) _____ doors. These keys were curved bars. Some of them were over three feet long and were (14) _____ over the shoulder.

13. (A) trapped	(B) unlock	(C) used	(D) wrapped
14. (A) wheeled	(B) marched	(C) stamped	(D) carried

Prairie dogs have air raid systems in their towns. A constant watch is kept on the skies. As soon as a hawk is sighted, a warning (15) _____ is (16) _____. All the prairie dogs rush underground until the danger passes.

15. (A) flag	(B) whistle	(C) gate	(D) look
16. (A) beaten	(B) thrown	(C) found	(D) sounded

The blue whale is a huge animal. Its heart weighs 800 pounds. Its tongue alone weighs as much as three automobiles! The whale is truly a (17) _____ of (18) _____.

17. (A) banana	(B) note	(C) cake	(D) giant
18. (A) prevention	(B) corner	(C) nest	(D) creation

When the explorers Lewis and Clark went west, they took a Shoshone Indian woman with them. Sacagawea was most (19) _____ to their expedition. As their guide, she showed them the wilderness, and she (20) _____ to the other tribes they met along the way.

19. (A) helpless	(B) scared	(C) helpful	(D) babyish
20. (A) left	(B) drove	(C) stayed	(D) spoke

Did you ever think of food having contexts just as words do? For example, people usually eat different kinds of foods at different meals. For breakfast, you might eat cereal, eggs, or pancakes. For lunch, you might have a sandwich or soup and a salad. For dinner, you might have some kind of meat, potatoes, and cooked vegetables. If someone served you cereal for dinner, you might think it was out of context!

A. Exercising Your Skill

On your paper, write the headings below. Under each heading, write the names of foods that you often eat at each of these meals. What kinds of foods often appear in the same context?

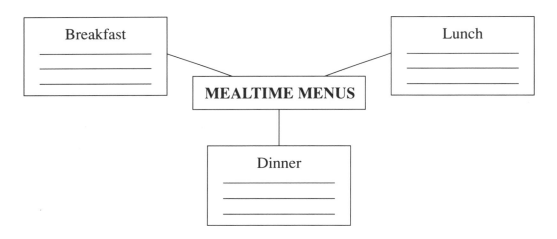

Do you eat snacks as well as these three meals? Write the heading "Snacks" on your paper, too. List the foods you eat as snacks.

B. Expanding Your Skill

You may want to compare your lists with your classmates' lists. Discuss the context in which each kind of food is served. Did some people in your class list foods you have never eaten? Use a dictionary to look up the names of foods you do not know. Write the names of new words related to foods that you learned by doing this activity.

C. Exploring Language

Use your own words to complete the following paragraphs. Write the paragraphs on your own paper. Give your story a title.

_____(Title)_____

    My favorite food is _____. I eat this food for _____. I like this food because _____. Some other foods I usually eat at the same meal are _____, _____, and _____.

    Let me describe how my favorite food looks, smells, and tastes. ____
_____
_____
_____

What do you think? Do you agree that _____ is the best food ever?

D. Expressing Yourself

Choose one of these activities.

1. Find a recipe for one of your favorite foods. If you cannot find a recipe, list the things you think would be in the food and tell how you think it would be made. Share your recipe with a classmate.

2. Work together with several classmates to plan a meal. Write a menu that shows what foods will be served. Then make a shopping list for the things you would have to buy to make this meal.

3. Use an encyclopedia or other reference book to find out about one of your favorite foods. Find the answers to these questions: Where does it come from? If it is a vegetable or fruit, how does it grow (bush, tree, vine, root)? In what countries is this food popular? Think of your own questions and find the answers.

Have you ever taken a trip and wished later that you could (1) _____ more about it? Eleanor Green has a good idea. She sends picture postcards home to herself with dates, times, and special (2) _____ for remembering the scenes pictured.

1. (A) imitate   (B) wrinkle   (C) remember   (D) litter
2. (A) gloves   (B) diseases   (C) oxygen   (D) reasons

Drop the most modern lightbulb. It won't break. It is coated with plastic. The shatterproof bulb can fall to a hard (3) _____ without exploding into a shower of (4) _____.

3. (A) surface   (B) sky   (C) jelly   (D) cloud
4. (A) rain   (B) glass   (C) gas   (D) jelly

Goldfish can live a fairly long life. If properly (5) _____ for, most goldfish live up to seventeen years. But there is a (6) _____ of one goldfish that lived to the ripe old age of forty!

5. (A) fished   (B) cared   (C) spoken   (D) ready
6. (A) record   (B) circle   (C) fold   (D) meal

A smiter was a person who worked with metal. The smiter would strike or "smite" the metal into the forms needed. In time, the word was (7) _____ and a metal (8) _____ became known as a "smith."

7. (A) changed   (B) spelled   (C) written   (D) bet
8. (A) doctor   (B) bird   (C) worker   (D) butterfly

Long ago there were no snowplows. Most roads didn't get cleared. The people with (9) _____ put them into (10) _____ for the winter. They were just as glad to go back to the horse and sled.

9. (A) coats   (B) pets   (C) dreams   (D) cars
10. (A) garages   (B) cellars   (C) stores   (D) kennels

New road signs are being made of rubber. If cars run into them by mistake, the damage is small. The signs just (11) _____ and return to their (12) _____ positions.

11. **(A) break**　　　**(B) smile**　　　**(C) cry**　　　**(D) bend**
12. **(A) strange**　　**(B) boxing**　　**(C) original**　　**(D) funny**

Pity the mail carrier who often has to face savage dogs that owners keep as "friendly" pets. In the past year alone, over six thousand mail carriers were bitten. Delivering (13) _____ is not without (14) _____.

13. **(A) mail**　　　**(B) milk**　　　**(C) wagons**　　**(D) time**
14. **(A) risks**　　　**(B) air**　　　　**(C) water**　　**(D) falls**

Some people have left their money to their horses. A Mrs. Snow willed $32,000 for the (15) _____ of her horses after her death, and a Mrs. Munro left $100,000 to her 32-year-old carriage horse (16) _____ Daisy.

15. **(A) country**　　**(B) speed**　　**(C) care**　　　**(D) news**
16. **(A) treated**　　**(B) named**　　**(C) promised**　**(D) aged**

In the early days, all written messages were like secret codes. Very few people were able to read or write. As time went on and more people learned to (17) _____, written messages were no longer a (18) _____.

17. **(A) sleep**　　　**(B) read**　　　**(C) walk**　　　**(D) swim**
18. **(A) mystery**　　**(B) city**　　　**(C) street**　　**(D) like**

Elephants love water. They spray each other until their wrinkled hides look black and shiny. Elephants make loud noises as they play in the water. They have as much (19) _____ as (20) _____ under a garden hose.

19. **(A) fear**　　　**(B) love**　　　**(C) time**　　　**(D) fun**
20. **(A) children**　　**(B) cars**　　　**(C) snakes**　　**(D) grass**

The roar of thunder may mean trouble for a cowhand. The booming noise often frightens the cattle. This causes the herd to scatter. Then the cowhand must (1) _____ on a horse to (2) _____ them up.

1. (A) follow   (B) talk   (C) swim   (D) spit
2. (A) round   (B) wind   (C) ask   (D) blow

Playing the bagpipes can take one's breath away. Donald Dobbie of Scotland (3) _____ this out when he played the pipes for twelve hours, then continued to play them on a seven-mile walk. He (4) _____ of exhaustion.

3. (A) drummed   (B) printed   (C) found   (D) borrowed
4. (A) swam   (B) died   (C) starved   (D) drilled

If you have a taste for rattlesnake steaks or fried bees, they are available. Think twice before you ask, "What's new for dinner?" The (5) _____ may (6) _____ you!

5. (A) ice   (B) answer   (C) city   (D) lizard
6. (A) kiss   (B) dry   (C) surprise   (D) sweep

The loneliest jump in the world is one taken from an airplane. Down, down toward the earth hurtles the (7) _____. How (8) _____ it seems before the sharp tug of the parachute says, "All is well."

7. (A) farmer   (B) jumper   (C) music   (D) firefighter
8. (A) funny   (B) long   (C) clean   (D) dirty

Nobody wants to get sick while traveling. Doctors give shots against certain (9) _____ to people going to some countries. They also tell travelers to drink bottled or boiled liquids. Dentists suggest that people have their (10) _____ checked before leaving.

9. (A) weights   (B) diseases   (C) worries   (D) tickets
10. (A) fur   (B) chimneys   (C) teeth   (D) humor

Would you like to eat a dish of chopped violets? Or a tulip stuffed with crabmeat? (11) _____ experts suggest we try eating certain (12) _____. Many people would be unwilling, but isn't it worth a try?

11. **(A) Plant**	**(B) Egg**	**(C) Cart**	**(D) Moon**
12. **(A) desserts**	**(B) flowers**	**(C) meats**	**(D) fruits**

A pet box turtle left home one day. Its sad owners (13) _____ for weeks for their brown turtle with the special gold (14) _____ on its back. Almost ten years later, the turtle returned to its owners' backyard!

13. **(A) knocked**	**(B) reminded**	**(C) searched**	**(D) spanked**
14. **(A) birds**	**(B) curtains**	**(C) locks**	**(D) marks**

It's lucky that mother whales don't have to carry their babies around. A baby whale might (15) _____ as much as five automobiles and (16) _____ twenty-five feet in length.

15. **(A) weigh**	**(B) speed**	**(C) start**	**(D) fly**
16. **(A) follow**	**(B) cut**	**(C) splash**	**(D) measure**

Icebergs are strangely beautiful to behold. Blue and green in color, they often tower hundreds of feet upward. When they float into warm water, they (17) _____ and finally (18) _____.

17. **(A) hide**	**(B) grow**	**(C) melt**	**(D) sing**
18. **(A) walk**	**(B) drown**	**(C) float**	**(D) disappear**

Long ago the falcon was used for hunting. This bird was trained to sit on the wrist of its owner until a duck was spotted. The falcon then darted away, soon to (19) _____ with its limp (20) _____.

19. **(A) cry**	**(B) return**	**(C) shout**	**(D) beg**
20. **(A) rags**	**(B) question**	**(C) victim**	**(D) tiger**

Throughout the year, visitors flock to Washington, D.C. to see the (1) _____ building and other points of (2) _____. They do not, however, see the tallest capitol building in the country. The tallest capitol building is in Austin, Texas.

1. (A) capitol   (B) brownstone   (C) tepee   (D) canyon
2. (A) spirit   (B) interest   (C) swords   (D) collection

Look closely at a stamp and you will see that it is really a small poster. Just like a poster, each stamp has a message, or (3) _____ to (4) _____.

3. (A) train   (B) doctor   (C) story   (D) fight
4. (A) glad   (B) call   (C) play   (D) tell

Perhaps you know what the official flower of your state is, but do you know what the (5) _____ flower of the United States is? If you guessed the rose, you guessed (6) _____!

5. (A) foreign   (B) mechanical   (C) unusual   (D) national
6. (A) halfway   (B) correctly   (C) terrible   (D) falsely

Some lizards throw away their tails to escape capture. With a sudden twist, off goes the tail. Around and around jumps the tail, as if alive! The (7) _____ chases the tail, and the clever lizard crawls away to (8) _____.

7. (A) enemy   (B) friend   (C) bush   (D) ear
8. (A) heaven   (B) die   (C) safety   (D) cry

A snow fence is made of wood. It is placed along highways. When the winter winds blow, the snow piles up against the (9) _____ instead of blowing all over the (10) _____.

9. (A) car   (B) sun   (C) garage   (D) fence
10. (A) truck   (B) tide   (C) river   (D) road

Mustard certainly adds flavor to food. Long ago, mustard served a different purpose. Used as a medicine, it was thought to be (11) _____ enough to burn out any (12) _____ .

11. (A) lovely   (B) hot   (C) gentle   (D) large
12. (A) pink   (B) forest   (C) pain   (D) fire

The porcupine is an excellent swimmer. This is not surprising. It has a built-in life jacket. Every one of its pointed quills is (13) _____ and filled with (14) _____ .

13. (A) pretty   (B) boots   (C) solid   (D) hollow
14. (A) food   (B) air   (C) dreams   (D) hands

An unusual hen in South America lays eggs of all colors! Its owner can never be certain just what colors the eggs will be. (15) _____ eggs for (16) _____ are no problem here.

15. (A) Drain   (B) Soft   (C) Wet   (D) Colored
16. (A) Easter   (B) dinner   (C) breakfast   (D) troubles

Have you ever wondered if a fish sleeps? It does, usually many times a day. It is difficult, though, to tell when a fish is asleep, since it has no (17) _____ to (18) _____ .

17. (A) train   (B) door   (C) eyelids   (D) eye
18. (A) turn   (B) think   (C) rest   (D) close

The Incas built a highway through the clouds. This road runs over (19) _____ 14,000 feet high. Even though it was built thousands of (20) _____ ago, some parts of it are still used by automobiles today.

19. (A) valleys   (B) trees   (C) mountains   (D) fountains
20. (A) years   (B) days   (C) workers   (D) miles

The first Ferris wheel was probably the biggest one ever (1) _____. It was put up in Chicago in 1893. Over a thousand people could be (2) _____ in its thirty-six cars.

1. (A) knelt   (B) spoken   (C) tasted   (D) built
2. (A) smoked   (B) seated   (C) galloped   (D) accused

A woodpecker is very fast at pecking. The bird can peck at the wood of a (3) _____ trunk twenty times in a second and can do this for nearly an hour at a (4) _____. That's more than seventy thousand times in one hour.

3. (A) metal   (B) youth   (C) tree   (D) elephant
4. (A) shock   (B) stretch   (C) clatter   (D) pillow

Few groups of people have had as colorful names as the Native Americans from the North. "Dull Knife," "Crazy Horse," "Red Cloud," and "Sitting Bull" are just a (5) _____ of the (6) _____ that will live on in history.

5. (A) never   (B) few   (C) cowhand   (D) color
6. (A) kind   (B) person   (C) names   (D) ladies

Some small fish stay near shore when the tide goes out. They often (7) _____ in puddles beneath rocks. Here they can swim in safety until the (8) _____ comes in again.

7. (A) run   (B) hide   (C) chew   (D) wave
8. (A) boat   (B) seed   (C) tide   (D) seaweed

No matches are needed to light safety candles. The "flames" are made of plastic. They light by means of batteries. Churches and schools (9) _____ safety (10) _____ for important services and events.

9. (A) throw   (B) worship   (C) wave   (D) use
10. (A) parties   (B) gift   (C) clubs   (D) candles

Can you imagine six feet of snow falling in just one day? It happened in Silver Lake, Colorado, many years ago. What if a snowstorm like that were to (11) _____ for a (12) _____?

| 11. | (A) shovel | (B) last | (C) bottle | (D) mask |
| 12. | (A) week | (B) laugh | (C) sled | (D) chance |

Ida Lewis was the daughter of the keeper of the Lime Rock Lighthouse in Rhode Island. When she was sixteen, she (13) _____ four boys from drowning. When she was sixty-four, she made her twenty-third (14) _____.

| 13. | (A) blew | (B) saved | (C) wrote | (D) taught |
| 14. | (A) century | (B) speech | (C) wish | (D) rescue |

Many people live in houses with "legs." Those who live in stilt houses say the (15) _____ is better and that there is less danger of (16) _____. They also say that these houses are cooler.

| 15. | (A) view | (B) much | (C) danger | (D) tramp |
| 16. | (A) floods | (B) armies | (C) airplane | (D) travel |

The ancient Romans had saltwater farms. They fenced off areas of the sea. Inside these areas, they (17) _____ the (18) _____. When the fish were large enough, they were netted for the table.

| 17. | (A) fed | (B) starved | (C) fried | (D) kissed |
| 18. | (A) area | (B) grass | (C) seeds | (D) fish |

You have probably seen a dog swim but what about a rabbit? A rabbit can also swim if it needs to. A rabbit being (19) _____ will swim across a (20) _____. Rabbits living in wet swamps and marshes swim much of the time.

| 19. | (A) introduced | (B) explained | (C) chased | (D) reminded |
| 20. | (A) phone | (B) stream | (C) movie | (D) kennel |

False teeth are not a new idea. They were used thousands of years ago in Rome and Egypt. In those days (1) _____ teeth for people were made from dog's teeth or soft (2) _____.

1. (A) baby   (B) false   (C) real   (D) colored
2. (A) wood   (B) cotton   (C) water   (D) cardboard

How much money do Americans spend on pet food each year? Believe it or not, Americans spend one-and-a-half billion (3) _____ a year just to (4) _____ their pets. This is almost four times the sum spent on baby food.

3. (A) dollars   (B) echoes   (C) dozen   (D) flavors
4. (A) fetch   (B) feed   (C) clip   (D) polish

We think of snowflakes as dainty little things. Had we lived in Montana in 1887, we would have a completely different (5) _____. One snowflake that (6) _____ there was over a foot wide and six inches thick!

5. (A) idea   (B) house   (C) suit   (D) smell
6. (A) swam   (B) heard   (C) walked   (D) fell

You can tell the temperature if you listen to the chirp of a cricket. Just (7) _____ the number of chirps in fourteen seconds and add forty. That will be the temperature in Fahrenheit. The cricket is a (8) _____ thermometer.

7. (A) grab   (B) twist   (C) spin   (D) count
8. (A) living   (B) store   (C) costly   (D) cake

Arnold and Lisa are known as the king and queen of muscle. They say body building can (9) _____ people get into better (10) _____. Lisa is in such good condition that she can lift Arnold!

9. (A) scare   (B) help   (C) choke   (D) imagine
10. (A) shape   (B) luck   (C) noise   (D) thirst

The modern safe has a time lock. Bank robbers must not only learn the combination of the lock, but must find out the time for which the lock has been set. At no other (11) _____ can the safe be (12) _____.

11. (A) street   (B) time   (C) end   (D) trip
12. (A) built   (B) opened   (C) told   (D) cooked

An unusual kind of rope is now for sale. Made of rubber, it stretches to four times its original size. What a bargain! When you buy one foot, you get four (13) _____ your money's (14) _____.

13. (A) times   (B) days   (C) drops   (D) wheels
14. (A) less   (B) worth   (C) color   (D) candy

In colonial days, children played tag, marbles, and leapfrog. Kites and tops were popular playthings. Don't these games and toys make you think more of the (15) _____ than of the (16) _____?

15. (A) window   (B) night   (C) present   (D) winter
16. (A) door   (B) sky   (C) past   (D) minute

The Victoria Gate in Dundee, Scotland, was built in 1844 to honor Queen Victoria of England. The Queen visited there for only one day, but the memorial to her has (17) _____ for over 140 (18) _____.

17. (A) smiled   (B) remained   (C) moved   (D) died
18. (A) miles   (B) questions   (C) years   (D) points

It was once thought that camels would make good letter carriers. Seventy-five of them were brought to America. Since the heavy mail sacks made the camels (19) _____, the experiment was a (20) _____.

19. (A) laugh   (B) cold   (C) angry   (D) swim
20. (A) dish   (B) failure   (C) dance   (D) rocket

Can you imagine a pumpkin weighing more than 600 pounds? Norman Gallagher (1) _____ one in Chelan, Washington. He won a grand (2) _____ of $10,000 and a one-week trip to Hawaii.

1. (A) lost   (B) raised   (C) dug   (D) drew
2. (A) march   (B) title   (C) stand   (D) prize

Did you know that you're a little taller in the morning than you are at night? Your backbone is stretched to its full (3) _____ in the morning. All day the weight of your body pushes on your backbone making it and you (4) _____ .

3. (A) length   (B) sorrow   (C) breath   (D) shade
4. (A) fearless   (B) shorter   (C) homeless   (D) happier

Shells found along the seashore were once the homes of sea creatures. Maybe you can tell which animals used to live in the shells you find. Collecting shells of different (5) _____ and colors is an interesting (6) _____ .

5. (A) storms   (B) seasons   (C) nuts   (D) shapes
6. (A) hobby   (B) story   (C) person   (D) trip

To keep hounds quiet, they were given bits of unsweetened cornmeal fried in deep fat. (7) _____ to a (8) _____ , this was the origin of the southern dish that came to be known as "hush puppies."

7. (A) Building   (B) Reading   (C) Waiting   (D) According
8. (A) legend   (B) soldier   (C) dog   (D) vote

Cowhands liked to sing. They made up songs about their homes and their sweethearts. Sometimes they sang of the wide open spaces or of the deaths of brave cowhands. Their (9) _____ kept them from becoming (10) _____ .

9. (A) guns   (B) stars   (C) wagon   (D) songs
10. (A) deaf   (B) strong   (C) flowers   (D) lonesome

People in the South Seas Islands say "hello" by throwing themselves on the ground. To them, this means respect and friendship. In our country, we greet friends with a smile or a (11) _____ of the (12) _____ .

11. **(A) smell**   **(B) kick**   **(C) shake**   **(D) smack**
12. **(A) tongue**   **(B) hand**   **(C) tie**   **(D) ankle**

Have you ever worked on a maze? The word *maze* (13) _____ "to lose one's senses." The purpose of a maze is not to really drive you crazy, but to confuse you and (14) _____ you. Have fun doing your next maze!

13. **(A) comes**   **(B) means**   **(C) asks**   **(D) wants**
14. **(A) sadden**   **(B) anger**   **(C) wake**   **(D) amuse**

Have you ever heard of a "fair-weather" friend? Although near when things are going well for you, a fair-weather friend usually (15) _____ when trouble or (16) _____ weather comes your way.

15. **(A) sings**   **(B) lifts**   **(C) runs**   **(D) talks**
16. **(A) sunny**   **(B) stormy**   **(C) red**   **(D) friendly**

Cooks of long ago were very skillful. They could make pork taste like game birds, and turnips taste like fish. In England, a cook was considered an (17) _____ if the guests did not (18) _____ what they had eaten.

17. **(A) expert**   **(B) echo**   **(C) aunt**   **(D) animal**
18. **(A) know**   **(B) want**   **(C) wolf**   **(D) stand**

Colors affect our feelings and moods. It might be well to consider this before you (19) _____ your room. To most people, yellow is cheerful, red is exciting, and blue is peaceful. Which (20) _____ is right for you?

19. **(A) close**   **(B) hit**   **(C) paint**   **(D) find**
20. **(A) suit**   **(B) color**   **(C) door**   **(D) window**

UNIT 19

Is the biggest number you can think of a million or a billion? Scientists know there are always bigger numbers and use the (1) _____ ∞ to show that numbers never end. The largest number with a (2) _____ is a "googol"—1 with 100 zeros after it.

1. (A) visitor   (B) symbol   (C) order   (D) year
2. (A) name   (B) ship   (C) fan   (D) cork

An underwater volcano in the Pacific Ocean may develop into a new (3) _____ near Hawaii. The volcano keeps getting bigger. Scientists won't guess how long it will take the new island to rise out of the (4) _____.

3. (A) custom   (B) island   (C) dessert   (D) paragraph
4. (A) society   (B) jungle   (C) ocean   (D) brush

You may have seen, or even run into a swarm of (5) _____ or a pack of wolves. But have you been aware that a group of elks is (6) _____ a gang, and that a group of crows is known as a murder?

5. (A) crowds   (B) bees   (C) wind   (D) music
6. (A) carried   (B) crushed   (C) called   (D) poisoned

When we want to say that something is extremely thick, we use the expression, "as thick as an elephant's hide." It is a fact that elephants sometimes have (7) _____ that is an inch and a half (8) _____.

7. (A) heads   (B) skin   (C) feet   (D) trunks
8. (A) red   (B) thick   (C) lost   (D) taken

Have you ever watched with wonder as birds gracefully dip and dive into the water? Some birds are real deep-sea divers. They can (9) _____ down over a hundred feet and come up again without (10) _____.

9. (A) dive   (B) chop   (C) shovel   (D) sink
10. (A) fish   (B) difficulty   (C) crying   (D) seaweed

There is a scale so perfectly balanced that it can weigh a human hair. It can even weigh the writing on a piece of paper. You will certainly (11) _____ that it is a remarkable (12) _____.

11. (A) balance   (B) agree   (C) weigh   (D) dislike
12. (A) instrument   (B) animal   (C) man   (D) paper

The famous "Quaker Cannons" of the Civil War were not cannons at all. They were logs painted black, made to look like cannons. They often fooled the enemy, but a single (13) _____ was never (14) _____ from them.

13. (A) person   (B) worker   (C) dog   (D) shot
14. (A) laughed   (B) fooled   (C) fired   (D) look

American elevators probably travel close to a hundred million miles a year. The elevators, if they could talk, might well add, "But we don't (15) _____ to be (16) _____ anywhere—just up and down!"

15. (A) crack   (B) crash   (C) hate   (D) seem
16. (A) going   (B) trying   (C) swimming   (D) found

Mountain climbers are (17) _____ what happens to the human body as they climb. Since their bodies get less oxygen as they go higher, they are learning to deal with diseases in which there are low levels of (18) _____ in the blood.

17. (A) shoveling   (B) braving   (C) studying   (D) muttering
18. (A) noise   (B) oxygen   (C) salt   (D) sugar

When it rains, water runs down into the soil and fills up all the air spaces. Earthworms come up for air. Notice how many worms are out (19) _____ the next time it (20) _____.

19. (A) flying   (B) crawling   (C) sunning   (D) teeth
20. (A) rains   (B) closes   (C) snows   (D) passes

47

Rowing is a popular sport at many high schools and colleges. Rowing is divided into two types of races, <u>regattas</u> and <u>head of the river</u> races. Regattas are held on both rivers and lakes. Head races are held on rivers. Racing <u>shells</u> are long, slim, lightweight boats. Races are held for singles and pairs. In <u>sculling</u> each person uses two <u>sculls</u>, or oars. In rowing, each <u>rower</u> uses one oar. Races are held for pairs, fours, and eights.

A. Exercising Your Skill

When you read the paragraph above, you may not have known the meanings of the underlined words, but you could tell a great deal about them from the context. For one thing, you could tell that they were on the subject of rowing. You could also use context clues to figure out the meanings of the words. Some words are explained in the same or a nearby sentence. *Synonyms*, or words with similar meanings, are another context clue.

On your paper, write each underlined word. Next to each word, write its meaning. Tell what clues you used to figure out each word's meaning.

B. Expanding Your Skill

Other words related to rowing include *coxswain, course, umpire, starter, aligner,* and *bow.* Use a dictionary or other reference books to find out the meanings of these words as they relate to rowing. Write the words and their meanings on your own paper.

C. Exploring Language

You have seen some ways in which context helped show the meanings of special words used in a sport. Write complete sentences for three of the words from Part B. Include context clues that will help a reader figure out the meanings of the special words.

Exchange your sentences with a classmate. As you read each other's sentences, see if you can figure out the meanings of the special words by using the context.

D. Expressing Yourself

Choose one of these activities.

1. Imagine that you are a reporter attending a regatta. Write a news article about the race. Include some of the special terms related to rowing, and be sure to use context clues to help your readers.

2. Use reference books to find out what a racing shell looks like. Draw a diagram of a shell, labeling all of its parts. Show the diagram to your class. See if your classmates can tell you what each part does by looking at the diagram. Tell them if their answers are right or wrong.

3. Choose a sport you enjoy playing or watching. Write a paragraph to tell others about this sport. Be sure to include context clues to help define any special terms you use in your paragraph.

The Dead Sea is really a lake between Israel and Jordan. It is saltier than any other body of water. Fish and most kinds of (1) _____ die from all the salt. That's why it's called the (2) _____ Sea.

1. (A) rocks   (B) plants   (C) ships   (D) sand
2. (A) Baltic   (B) Fresh   (C) Dead   (D) Suez

The thirteenth floor is missing in many hotels. Floor numbers jump from twelve to fourteen. Many people think the (3) _____ thirteen is unlucky. They would (4) _____ to take a room on the thirteenth floor.

3. (A) letter   (B) color   (C) number   (D) lady
4. (A) fight   (B) refuse   (C) forget   (D) try

People who like to (5) _____ can find sweets in Hershey, Pennsylvania, nicknamed the Chocolate Capital of the World. For pretzels and peanuts, they can (6) _____ Pretzel City (Reading, Pennsylvania) and Peanut City (Suffolk, Virginia).

5. (A) fight   (B) swim   (C) skate   (D) snack
6. (A) avoid   (B) leave   (C) visit   (D) miss

Children like dandelions. They can whistle through the hollow stems or braid a necklace of golden flowers. Adults think of dandelions as (7) _____ instead of (8) _____. They are annoyed to find them growing in lawns.

7. (A) worms   (B) weeds   (C) trees   (D) baseballs
8. (A) flowers   (B) cars   (C) animals   (D) bats

In days gone by, a kiss was a common form of greeting. Visitors kissed everyone in the household, including the dog, cat, and the chickens! How (9) _____ do (10) _____!

9. (A) turnips   (B) rivers   (C) customs   (D) coins
10. (A) pick   (B) smile   (C) change   (D) walk

The sight of a Viking ship made even the bravest people (11) _____ with fear. The Vikings who sailed these ships were fierce sailors. Their attacks were certain to bring (12) _____ .

11 (A) tremble   (B) laugh   (C) sink   (D) heal
12. (A) trouble   (B) presents   (C) rain   (D) smiles

The human ear is truly amazing. It contains nerves that act like telephone wires. These nerves carry sounds. The human ear contains enough nerves to provide phone (13) _____ for an entire (14) _____ .

13. (A) books   (B) service   (C) poles   (D) bills
14. (A) desk   (B) hat   (C) city   (D) sentence

Plants are very helpful. They give off oxygen which (15) _____ and animals breathe. They supply fuel and medicine. And, above all, they are (16) _____ to look at.

15. (A) cactus   (B) evergreens (C) weeds   (D) people
16. (A) horrible   (B) beautiful   (C) ugly   (D) costly

You can (17) _____ the birthday of someone you love by having an American flag flown over the U.S. Capitol in Washington, D.C. You buy the flag which afterwards is sent to the birthday child along with a card telling the date it was (18) _____ and for whom.

17. (A) celebrate   (B) tighten   (C) ripen   (D) destroy
18. (A) burned   (B) drowned   (C) flown   (D) buried

How would you like to wash the windows of a New York skyscraper? The Chrysler Building has over 3,000 windows. The Empire State Building has 6,000. Sounds (19) _____ a full-time (20) _____ , doesn't it?

19. (A) silent   (B) like   (C) far   (D) blow
20. (A) garden   (B) job   (C) glass   (D) moon

The Taj Mahal in India is one of the most beautiful buildings in the world. Built by an Indian ruler in memory of his wife, the building is over three hundred years old. It (1) _____ many (2) _____.

1. (A) hides   (B) attracts   (C) scares   (D) lost

2. (A) babies   (B) insects   (C) visitors   (D) fish

The custom of giving Easter eggs is old. People in Egypt painted eggs thousands of years ago. They (3) _____ them during the new moon in April. The (4) _____ meant that life had returned to the earth.

3. (A) left   (B) ruined   (C) failed   (D) exchanged

4. (A) custom   (B) dust   (C) paper   (D) cupboard

In ten days, a tiny baby eats enough food to equal its own weight. An adult takes about five times as long to (5) _____ as much food as she or he (6) _____.

5. (A) sold   (B) frozen   (C) hide   (D) eat

6. (A) pays   (B) paints   (C) weighs   (D) looks

Do you know all the words of the three verses of the Star-Spangled Banner, our national anthem? It may seem like a lot to learn but don't (7) _____ too much. The national anthem of Greece (8) _____ 158 verses!

7. (A) quarrel   (B) complain   (C) borrow   (D) fasten

8. (A) turns   (B) drives   (C) contains   (D) breaks

Single steers that run away from a herd are often called "windies." Cowhands who try to overtake the "windies" are likely to be (9) _____ of (10) _____ before the job is done.

9. (A) silent   (B) time   (C) eat   (D) out

10. (A) dipper   (B) message   (C) wind   (D) rainbow

There are two good ways of getting the autograph of a famous person. You can try to meet the person and (11) _____ for a signature, or you can write to the person and request an (12) _____.

11. (A) scold   (B) ask   (C) trip   (D) shout
12. (A) money   (B) wallet   (C) autograph   (D) auto

"More and more (13) _____ are talking to you these days—including elevators, cars, and cameras," wrote Erma Bombeck. She suggested that a talking scale might (14) _____ someone who lost weight, or say to an overeater: "Will *one* of you please get off me?"

13. (A) colds   (B) blossoms   (C) products   (D) circles
14. (A) smell   (B) awaken   (C) surround   (D) praise

Some words say one thing but mean something else. Take the expression "Hold your horses." It doesn't (15) _____ you should keep a team of horses from moving. It does mean you should take your (16) _____ or be more patient.

15. (A) rush   (B) hold   (C) mean   (D) force
16. (A) angry   (B) nervous   (C) time   (D) money

The tumbleweed is a weed that grows on the prairie. When its stem breaks off, the wind carries it far, blowing its seeds across open (17) _____ and over (18) _____.

17. (A) windows   (B) doors   (C) fields   (D) mouths
18. (A) fences   (B) rugs   (C) icebergs   (D) chairs

Fish eggs can be expensive. Some cost $100 per pound. Called caviar, these eggs are (19) _____ in fine (20) _____. If you order caviar, be sure not to leave any of it on your plate!

19. (A) caught   (B) served   (C) made   (D) written
20. (A) restaurants (B) feelings   (C) times   (D) garages

A person living in the United States eats a lot of (1) _____. In a lifetime, it comes to about 150 cows, 225 lambs, 26 sheep, and 310 hogs. That same person also eats about 26 acres of grains and 50 acres of fruits and (2) _____.

1. **(A) meat**   **(B) chocolate**   **(C) questions**   **(D) cinnamon**
2. **(A) breads**   **(B) vegetables**   **(C) fish**   **(D) chicken**

A swallow can (3) _____ 2,000 mosquitoes each day. But the swallow is (4) _____ compared to the Maryland yellow bird. The yellow bird can gulp down 3,000 plant lice in little more than a half hour!

3. **(A) chase**   **(B) drown**   **(C) sting**   **(D) eat**
4. **(A) slow**   **(B) fast**   **(C) large**   **(D) heavy**

It has been said that lambswool causes dust to leap! That's why the wool of lambs is (5) _____ into dusters for furniture, china, lights, pictures, etc. Many lambswool dusters (6) _____ from New Zealand.

5. **(A) carried**   **(B) made**   **(C) drained**   **(D) grown**
6. **(A) shear**   **(B) wear**   **(C) come**   **(D) hunt**

Large and round as a huge beach ball, the sunfish is the "fatty" of the sea. It spends much time floating on the surface and sunning itself. It is easy to see how it (7) _____ its (8) _____.

7. **(A) lost**   **(B) got**   **(C) spent**   **(D) dropped**
8. **(A) friends**   **(B) hat**   **(C) money**   **(D) name**

The basilisk is a lively, South American lizard. When an enemy (9) _____ it, the basilisk stands up and runs on its long hind legs. It can run right across the surface of a stream. Its long toes keep it from (10) _____.

9. **(A) leaves**   **(B) approaches**   **(C) cares**   **(D) floats**
10. **(A) sinking**   **(B) running**   **(C) flying**   **(D) sitting**

You have probably heard of the famous Blarney Stone. It is located in a castle in Ireland. According to legend, those who kiss it become clever speakers, forever able to (11) _____ people with (12) _____.

11. (A) love   (B) charm   (C) dream   (D) wild
12. (A) words   (B) stones   (C) visits   (D) light

People used to believe that certain snakes visited barns in order to milk cows! It is true that snakes often visit barns, but they are looking for mice to (13) _____, not cows to (14) _____.

13. (A) fight   (B) squeal   (C) buy   (D) catch
14. (A) pet   (B) follow   (C) clean   (D) milk

Most people stop growing when they get to be twenty-one or twenty-two years of age. Movie star, Bess Armstrong, surprised everyone by (15) _____ a full inch at the (16) _____ of twenty-five.

15. (A) growing   (B) joining   (C) marching   (D) swallowing
16. (A) skin   (B) age   (C) size   (D) log

An elephant makes a shrill cry when taking a cool bath or while enjoying a tasty dinner. A roar means that something has angered it. The elephant has a (17) _____ that expresses its every (18) _____.

17. (A) friend   (B) voice   (C) tail   (D) tusks
18. (A) pole   (B) cent   (C) mood   (D) mouth

The Native Americans of the Great Plains didn't know any word to use as a greeting. They tried to copy the "howdy" that cowhands used. When they (19) _____ people, they would raise their hand and say, (20) _____.

19. (A) met   (B) knew   (C) walked   (D) left
20. (A) "How"   (B) "Silent"   (C) "Why"   (D) "Nothing"

Do you know someone who lives in a house on a corner? People who live on corners say their houses get (1) _____ of light and air. Corner houses are also easy to (2) _____. Corners show off the houses.

1. (A) lack   (B) plenty   (C) aimless   (D) unkind
2. (A) fight   (B) find   (C) curl   (D) prove

Some say the sand dunes of the desert look like ocean waves. Others think the dunes look like mounds of snow. People living in desert regions must often wish the dunes really were (3) _____ or (4) _____.

3. (A) egg   (B) water   (C) air   (D) metal
4. (A) fog   (B) dunes   (C) snow   (D) salt

New Year's Day has not always been the first of January. Over one thousand years ago, it was a spring holiday. People used to think a new year should begin with (5) _____ instead of (6) _____.

5. (A) hate   (B) sign   (C) spring   (D) lies
6. (A) winter   (B) lump   (C) group   (D) summer

How old is that pretty glass bowl? From the time it was made, a thin crust has formed on its surface each year. By (7) _____ the (8) _____, the age of the glass bowl can be figured.

7. (A) counting   (B) selling   (C) ignoring   (D) eating
8. (A) tree   (B) layers   (C) weather   (D) knuckles

People with stomach trouble are sometimes asked to swallow the "radio pill." This pill will send radio beams from the stomach to the doctor. From the beams, the doctor can gain information to (9) _____ treat the (10) _____.

9. (A) trips   (B) prevents   (C) help   (D) ride
10. (A) car   (B) patient   (C) radio   (D) sky

UNIT 23

Study the different parts of your fingers and see how they move. During a lifetime, the various parts of a person's fingers move 25 million (11) _____. If you play the (12) _____ or type a lot, they move even more times than that.

11. (A) facts   (B) zones   (C) times   (D) verbs
12. (A) judge   (B) piano   (C) leader   (D) toy

Allison Herdan has an unusual hobby. She (13) _____ labels from clothes. Whenever she buys something new, she (14) _____ off the label with the trade name and keeps it. Many labels have interesting designs on them.

13. (A) misses   (B) collects   (C) mails   (D) forgets
14. (A) climbs   (B) cuts   (C) wheels   (D) sounds

The Klondike gold rush of 1897 attracted thousands of people who thought they would get (15) _____. Of the 20,000 who set out for the gold fields, only a few thousand found any (16) _____ at all.

15. (A) butter   (B) poor   (C) rich   (D) sick
16. (A) coal   (B) gold   (C) silver   (D) copper

An egg is slightly more pointed at one end than the other. Nature has a good reason for this. Perfectly round eggs are more likely to roll out of a (17) _____ nest than are the (18) _____ ones.

17. (A) shallow   (B) hill   (C) strong   (D) deep
18. (A) blue   (B) yellow   (C) pointed   (D) fat

It's no wonder that farmers are always looking for rain. One hundred pounds of rainwater are needed to (19) _____ a single pound of food. More than ten tons of water must (20) _____ over an acre of corn plants to grow one bushel of corn.

19. (A) claw   (B) grow   (C) glow   (D) stripe
20. (A) fall   (B) fail   (C) hush   (D) flock

UNIT 24

One out of every ten people in China (1) _____ a bicycle. The Chinese have bikes with sidecars for children, (2) _____ for chickens, and they even have a "school bus" which takes as many as eight to a day-care center.

1. (A) rides   (B) visits   (C) plows   (D) bathes
2. (A) alphabets   (B) cages   (C) pencils   (D) oars

One person owns an unusual pet. It is a fish that changes color each time it sees food! Scientists cannot explain what causes this. Perhaps the excitement of (3) _____ food somehow affects the (4) _____ color of the fish.

3. (A) bake   (B) bait   (C) drinking   (D) seeing
4. (A) skin   (B) ready   (C) dirty   (D) dead

People forget most of what they read a very short time afterwards. It has been said that more than eighty percent is (5) _____ in two weeks. Chances are that you will (6) _____ what you are now reading.

5. (A) forgotten   (B) think   (C) trimmed   (D) correct
6. (A) tell   (B) forget   (C) trip   (D) listen

When a cowhand said, "Let's vamoose," to a friend, it meant "Let's get going!" When it was said to an enemy, it meant "Get out!" or "Move on!" People who (7) _____ usually go away (8) _____.

7. (A) validate   (B) vamoose   (C) sing   (D) walk
8. (A) friendly   (B) quickly   (C) sleeping   (D) tried

Why not try walking on water? The new "water shoes" make it possible for you to walk right on the surface. You will think nothing of walking across a (9) _____ fully (10) _____.

9. (A) street   (B) wire   (C) lake   (D) bridge
10. (A) sink   (B) clothed   (C) empty   (D) tired

Secret messages were once written on the forehead of a trusted messenger! Hair was allowed to grow until the (11) _____ was (12) _____. Upon arriving, the messenger's hair was cut and the message read.

11. (A) chair   (B) pillow   (C) message   (D) news
12. (A) covered   (B) limp   (C) felt   (D) new

Many birds migrate, or move from place to place. The champion of them all is probably the Arctic tern. This bird spends its summer near the North Pole. When (13) _____ arrives, it (14) _____ to the South Pole, 10,000 miles away.

13. (A) rain   (B) food   (C) winter   (D) wind
14. (A) flies   (B) swims   (C) fishes   (D) runs

Barnacles like boats, but boats don't like barnacles. Fond of ocean liners, barnacles (15) _____ themselves to the bottoms. The speed of a liner is sometimes cut in half as millions of barnacles hang on for the (16) _____.

15. (A) seat   (B) leap   (C) attach   (D) throw
16. (A) speed   (B) ride   (C) stick   (D) light

Siberia, well-known for its cold weather, now claims to have had the (17) _____ snowflakes. In 1971, snowflakes were recorded that were the size of footballs. They (18) _____ nine inches across and nineteen inches in length!

17. (A) highest   (B) lowest   (C) newest   (D) largest
18. (A) measured   (B) fed   (C) baked   (D) believed

Have you ever heard of the wombat, a hairy-nosed animal of Australia? When it goes into its burrow, it uses its rear end to (19) _____ the burrow's opening and keep out (20) _____!

19. (A) admit   (B) cover   (C) straighten   (D) untie
20. (A) enemies   (B) words   (C) buildings   (D) ancestors

The Great Paper Boat Race of the World is (1) _____ each year in Port Hawkesbury, Nova Scotia, Canada. Anyone can enter. Boats must be made of paper, carry at least a three-person (2) _____, and be powered by wind or muscle (no motors).

1. (A) flown   (B) held   (C) spoken   (D) dug
2. (A) crew   (B) mast   (C) flight   (D) couple

Ground beneath the "crying tree" is always wet. The showers are caused by thousands of tiny insects which suck sap from the tree. Part of the sap is used as food. The rest (3) _____ like (4) _____.

3. (A) spins   (B) flies   (C) falls   (D) grows
4. (A) tops   (B) birds   (C) tears   (D) weeds

Pockets were once large bags tied to a belt. As time passed, pockets grew smaller. Then they were sewn right into the clothes. Pockets of (5) _____ do not (6) _____ as much as they once did.

5. (A) former   (B) today   (C) books   (D) then
6. (A) hold   (B) sell   (C) good   (D) feed

Did your eyes ever get sunburned? This can happen if you are climbing a steep mountain or walking on dazzling sand. By wearing dark (7) _____ you can (8) _____ your eyes from the sun.

7. (A) socks   (B) glasses   (C) ropes   (D) shoes
8. (A) clean   (B) harm   (C) follow   (D) protect

Many strange stories are told about snakes. The glass snake, for instance, is said to (9) _____ itself into (10) _____ when an enemy comes near. It puts itself together again when danger has passed.

9. (A) father   (B) person   (C) break   (D) warn
10. (A) love   (B) pieces   (C) leaps   (D) smoke

Two wheelchair racers traveled about 150 miles in 48 hours. They made the (11) _____ from Albany to New York City so that other people in wheelchairs would realize that it's (12) _____ to take part in sports.

11. (A) timber	**(B) trip**	**(C) movie**	**(D) supply**
12. (A) possible	**(B) hopeless**	**(C) impossible**	**(D) wicked**

A ten-ton vacuum cleaner is used on runways at airports. It sucks up objects that might (13) _____ an (14) _____. One thousand home vacuum cleaners would have to be used to do the same job.

13. (A) dark	**(B) dinner**	**(C) damage**	**(D) chill**
14. (A) crab	**(B) oven**	**(C) winter**	**(D) airplane**

Do you know what makes a jumping bean jump? It is the little (15) _____ that lives inside of it. Whenever the worm moves, the bean (16) _____ too. A jumping bean will continue to jump for three to four weeks.

15. (A) boy	**(B) worm**	**(C) clown**	**(D) joy**
16. (A) moves	**(B) recites**	**(C) mows**	**(D) soaks**

The Inuit people made masks to protect their eyes from the glare of the sun on the snow and ice. The masks were made of wood or bone. They had narrow slits for the (17) _____. Little sunlight could (18) _____ these slits.

17. (A) time	**(B) grass**	**(C) eyes**	**(D) beaver**
18. (A) chair	**(B) summer**	**(C) cheese**	**(D) enter**

Children played with dolls before the word "doll" was used. They called them puppets or babies. No matter what they were called, (19) _____ were and still are a (20) _____ plaything of children.

19. (A) tide	**(B) dolls**	**(C) race**	**(D) kiss**
20. (A) favorite	**(B) leaf**	**(C) end**	**(D) down**

Bird watching is a popular hobby. Some people can <u>gaze</u> for hours at birds. Most bird watchers are not much interested in birds like chickadees, which are <u>numerous</u>. Instead, they try to spot rare kinds that are <u>seldom</u> seen. Bird watchers try to learn the songs made by different birds. These songs are the way birds <u>communicate</u> with each other.

A. Exercising Your Skill

You may not have known the meanings of all the underlined words in the paragraph above, but you probably were able to figure them out from the context. The underlined words are in the questions below. Think about the meaning of each word. On your paper, write the words that answer the questions.

1. What can you <u>gaze</u> at?

trees	truth	rainbows
trust	people	clowns

2. Which things are <u>numerous</u>?

stars in the sky	hairs on your head
fish in the desert	people on the moon

3. Which things are <u>seldom</u> seen?

purple cows	children playing	birds flying
fish walking	snow in July	the sun

4. Which of these things are ways to <u>communicate</u>?

speaking	growling	sleeping
writing	eating	barking

B. Expanding Your Skill

With your classmates, discuss other examples of the underlined words. What else can you *gaze* at? What other things are *numerous* or *seldom* seen? Can you name other ways to *communicate*?

C. Exploring Language

Read each sentence and decide whether the underlined word makes sense. On your paper, write *yes* if the word is used correctly. Write *no* if it is not.

1. In the 1800s, serious bird watchers collected <u>specimens</u> of the different types of birds they saw.
2. Today, photographs of birds have <u>increased</u> the need to collect specimens.
3. Modern bird books give both photographs and written <u>descriptions</u> of birds.
4. Some types of birds are so <u>dissimilar</u> that it is hard to tell them apart.
5. Many birds <u>migrate</u>, flying to different homes in winter and summer.
6. Some birds have <u>considerable</u> ranges, while others live in narrower areas.

Look at the words that were used incorrectly. Use each word correctly in a sentence of your own. Try to include context clues to the word's meaning.

D. Expressing Yourself

Choose one of these activities.

1. Think of a bird that is common to your area. Describe it without using its name. See if your classmates can guess what bird you are describing.

2. Using old magazines, cut out pictures of birds. Find out the names of the birds and label them. Use a library book for help if you need it.